INNOCENT PRISONERS!
Life in a Japanese American Internment Camp

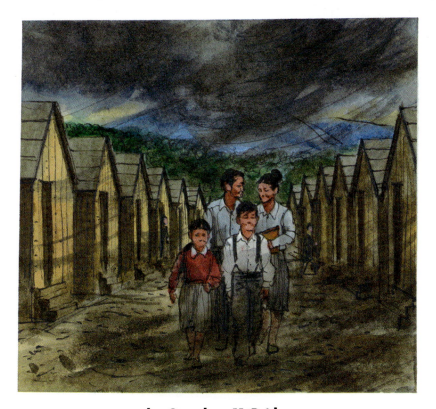

by Gretchen McBride
illustrated by Tom McNeely

Editorial Offices: Glenview, Illinois • Parsippany, New Jersey • New York, New York
Sales Offices: Needham, Massachusetts • Duluth, Georgia • Glenview, Illinois
Coppell, Texas • Ontario, California • Mesa, Arizona

Every effort has been made to secure permission and provide appropriate credit for photographic material. The publisher deeply regrets any omission and pledges to correct errors called to its attention in subsequent editions.

Unless otherwise acknowledged, all photographs are the property of Scott Foresman, a division of Pearson Education.

24 ©Susan Steinkamp/CORBIS

ISBN: 0-328-13420-1

Copyright © Pearson Education, Inc.

All Rights Reserved. Printed in the United States of America. This publication is protected by Copyright, and permission should be obtained from the publisher prior to any prohibited reproduction, storage in a retrieval system, or transmission in any form by any means, electronic, mechanical, photocopying, recording, or likewise. For information regarding permission(s), write to: Permissions Department, Scott Foresman, 1900 East Lake Avenue, Glenview, Illinois 60025.

7 8 9 10   V0G1   14 13 12 11 10 09 08

"When will we be able to go back to our farm in the San Fernando Valley, big brother?" Yukiko asked. She was Japanese, as were all the families in the camp.

"I don't know," said Aki. He spoke in Japanese, which was the language of their parents and the language they usually spoke at home. "Mama and Papa don't know."

Yukiko knew there was a war going on. She knew Japan had attacked Pearl Harbor, a naval base in Hawaii, on December 7, 1941. Since then, people in the United States treated their Japanese neighbors differently.

The U.S. government moved all Japanese and Japanese Americans to internment camps or relocation centers in early 1942 because of fears that they might become a threat to national security. The small rooms in the camps were called barracks. Every house was covered in tar paper, and there was no private kitchen or shower.

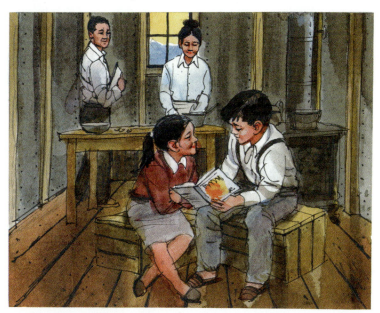

Yukiko went to find her father. She found him sitting outdoors on a chair he had made from scraps of wood. There wasn't enough furniture here, and people made their own from whatever they could find.

How was it possible the family had been living here for six whole months? "Come," said Papa to Yukiko. "Let's go get breakfast at the mess hall. We'll join the whole family there."

Everyone ate in the mess hall. Some families ate together, but many people now ate with the friends they had made at the camp. Yukiko liked sitting with her friends, but she missed the way her family used to eat in their own farmhouse. She even missed doing chores and helping out on the farm.

Yukiko knew Papa and Mama were not American citizens. But she and Aki were because they had been born in the United States. "Someday you will vote in elections!" Papa told them.

As the whole family sat at a big table together, Aki began telling a funny story he'd heard.

"Speak softly," Mama said. She was proud of her children's independent American ways, but she could not get used to the boisterous voices Americans used, and it was hard for her to understand their American speech.

Mama got up. "Aki, make sure your sister gets to school on time," she said.

"Where are you going, Mama?" Yukiko asked in Japanese, taking her mother's hand.

"Ah," Mama said with a private smile. "That is a secret I am keeping. Now do not be late for school."

After breakfast, Aki walked his sister to school, which was held in a small building across the dusty yard of the camp.

"Do you know what kind of secret Mama is keeping?" Yukiko asked. Aki shook his head.

"Are you going to be an American soldier after you graduate?" Yukiko asked Aki. Some of Aki's friends went away to fight in the war. Yukiko felt proud of them, but she was scared too. She loved America, but she didn't want Aki fighting any Japanese in the war.

"Here you go. Study hard," Aki said as he left Yukiko at school. The building was covered in dull black tar paper to keep out the dust. Yukiko missed the old two-story brick school building at home, and she missed her old classmates.

"Well, students, I have an exciting announcement to make!" the teacher said. "Some wonderful people have given our school another blackboard! It will be mounted on our classroom wall very soon."

Yukiko was quiet. Until now, her teacher had to write math problems on a piece of paper tacked to the wall. She thought how nice it would be to have a blackboard.

Yukiko wondered how people could be so nice sometimes, and other times be so mean. She had asked her father about this, but he merely shook his head. "It's wrong and unfair, but that is the way it is, and we cannot change it," he had said. Yukiko wanted a better answer.

After school, Yukiko met Aki in the yard. At this time of day, they always loved to look at Mount Whitney in the distance. Today they decided to walk to the edge of the camp, where they could get the best view of the mountain.

Although it felt good to walk after sitting at her school desk, Yukiko did not like the route they took. She hated seeing the barbed wire, the guard towers, and American soldiers holding real guns. Most of the time, she could pretend these things were not there. Sometimes she could even pretend that she and her family were living in a strange new town, but not now.

The wire and the guards made Yukiko feel as if she had done something wrong—they made her feel like a prisoner. But she and her family had done nothing wrong! The whole situation made her angry. How could her own government treat her and her family this way?

"Look at the beautiful mountain peaks!" said Aki.

Yukiko lifted her eyes to the horizon. There was snow-capped Mount Whitney towering above the desert. It really was breathtaking.

"I know the very best place to see the peak," Aki said. "Follow me!" They rounded a growth of sage brush. Then they stopped, amazed and bewildered. There, seated on a rock, was the oldest man Yukiko had ever seen.

The old man was sketching something on a large pad of paper. He looked up and saw them and gave them a big smile.

"Young ones," the old man said. "Before us is a great mountain—Mount Whitney! I come here often to admire it and to remember."

"Remember what?" asked Yukiko.

"This," the old man said, showing them his drawing. But it was not Mount Whitney. "This is Mount Fuji," the old man said. "It is in Japan, and it is sacred."

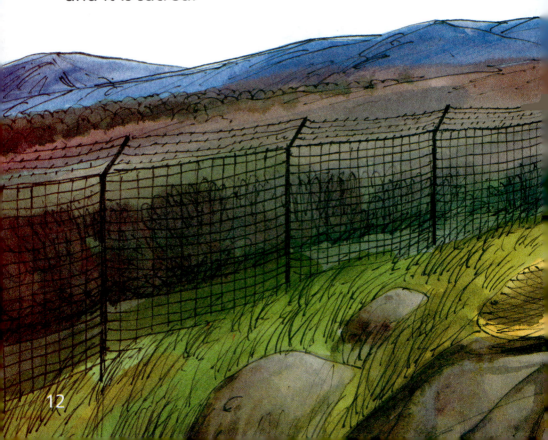

"Maybe after the war, you'll return to Japan," said Aki. "You can see Mount Fuji again."

"I will never return to Japan," sighed the old man. "I loved my homeland, but my life there was a hard one because we were poor. I urged my children to move to America for a better life, and they did. Soon, they sent for me."

He smiled sadly. "It is a mystery how we could all end up here behind these wires. I come here to think about this in the shadow of this great American mountain. It is now my Mount Fuji."

"Have you solved the mystery?" Aki asked. "Do you understand why we are here?"

"Ah," the old man said," I see that even you—so young—struggle with the mystery."

The old man smiled once more and handed Yukiko the drawing of Mount Fuji. Then he picked up his walking stick and slowly made his way along the dusty path back to the camp.

Aki and Yukiko walked a little and then stopped to gaze at the majestic snow-covered peak.

"Imagine," Aki said, "how clean the snow must be so far above the dust."

That evening at dinner, Aki sat with the older boys. That evening there were more complaints than usual about the hot dogs and beans.

Suddenly a man stood up. "When this is over, we need to turn our backs on the United States and go back to Japan!" he shouted.

"You are wrong! We are not Japanese. We are Japanese Americans! America is our home too," cried another man.

A shadow of a small woman fell across their table. It was Mama! "We must not disturb the peace of the other diners," she said in Japanese. "Let us all think hard about what is the right thing to do."

After dinner, the family walked back to their home. "Mother," Yukiko said suddenly, "what is your secret?"

This brought a smile to her mother's face. "Yukiko," she said, "what did you do in school today?"

The family looked at her in stunned silence. Finally, Aki spoke. "English! Mother, you spoke in English!"

"This is my secret," she said proudly. "I have no cooking to do, so I take class. I study English every morning."

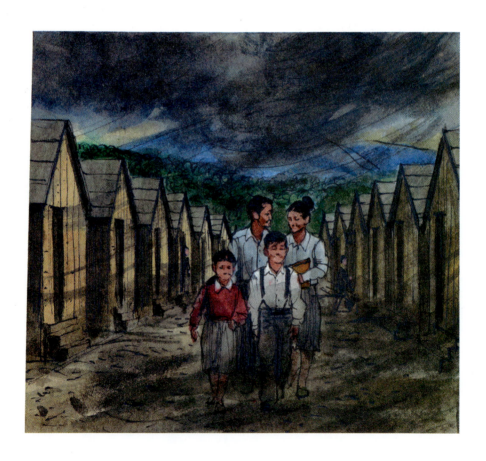

The wind began to blow the dust. "Another dust storm!" cried Aki. Talking was now impossible. Aki drew his jacket up to cover his nose and mouth with one hand. He put his other arm around Yukiko's shoulder.

Once inside the house, Father passed out rags. They pressed the rags into the cracks in the walls and the floor so the dust couldn't get in.

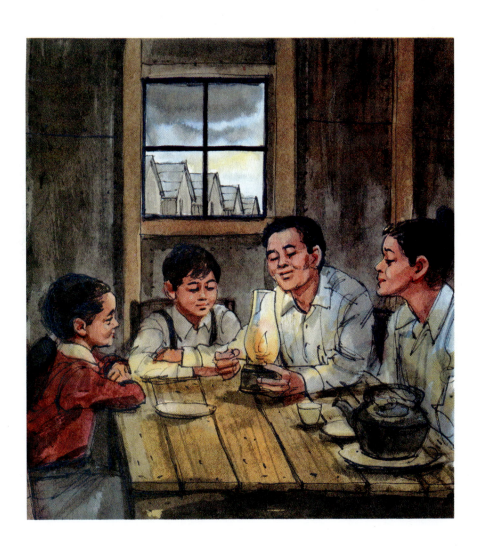

Three long years passed. Every year was harder than the one before. Yukiko felt as if they would never get out of the camp. And then, one morning, Yukiko heard great excitement outside. "The war is over! We're going home!" someone cried. Everyone was laughing and cheering.

Everyone gathered in the mess hall. Some people said they were going back to Japan. Other people wanted to go back to their American homes. But they were worried—would their homes still be there?

"What will we do?" Yukiko asked her parents.

"What do you want to do?" Father asked Yukiko. She thought long and hard. "I want to stay in America," she said. "This camp was a terrible thing. But this is still our country, isn't it?"

"I want to stay, too," said Mama. "It will be hard, but how else can I practice my English? I do not want to give up either language or either country. Someday, we will all visit Japan."

"I would like to see Mount Fuji," Yukiko said. She suddenly knew the first thing she would do when they got out of the camp and into a new home. She would hang the old man's drawing of Mount Fuji next to a drawing of Mount Whitney. Both mountains and both countries were important to her.

America Makes Amends

When the Japanese launched a surprise attack on the ships in Pearl Harbor, the United States was horrified. Japanese Americans were horrified too. But what horrified them more was how they were treated by some of their neighbors and by their own government. The Japanese were treated as if they were no longer Americans. They were treated as if they were to blame for the attack on Pearl Harbor.

The U.S. government, worried that they might be spies, put Japanese Americans into special camps called "relocation centers." After the war ended, the camps were closed. The last camp was closed in 1945.

Since that terrible time, America has realized that Japanese Americans were treated unjustly. In 1988, Congress gave money to every Japanese person who had been in a camp. In 1990, President George H. W. Bush sent letters of apology to them.